Going to Court

Sheila Hollins and Valerie Sinason
illustrated by Beth Webb

Beyond Words

London

3

First published in the UK 1994 by St George's Mental Health Library in association with VOICE (UK).

Second edition published 2016 by Books Beyond Words.

Text & illustrations © Books Beyond Words, 2016.

ISBN 978-1-78458-065-0

British Library Cataloguing-in-Publication Data
A catalogue record for this book is available from the British Library.

Printed by DX Imaging, Watford.

Books Beyond Words is a Community Interest Company registered in England and Wales (7557861).

Further information about the Books Beyond Words series can be obtained from Beyond Words' website: www.booksbeyondwords.co.uk.

Contents

Storyline

The following words are provided for readers and supporters who want some ideas about one possible story. Most readers make their own story up from the pictures.

1. Anita thinks a man did something wrong.

2. Anita's friend says, "We must call the police."

3. Anita's friend tells the police what happened.

4. A police officer comes to talk to Anita. Anita tells her what happened.

5. Police officers go to see the man she complained about.

6. They ask him to go to the police station.

7. Everything the man says is written down. It is also recorded on tape.

8. The police officers talk to a prosecutor. The prosecutor decides they should go to court.

9. Anita is given this book to tell her what will happen at court.

10. Anita reads the book.

11. Anita has to wait a long time.

12. Anita goes to see a court.

13. She talks to an usher who works at the court.

14. The usher shows her round the empty courtroom. Anita could go to watch someone else being a witness. That would help too.

15. Witnesses have to promise to tell the truth. Anita practises making the promise.

16. She keeps this book at home to help her think about going to court.

17. When the day comes Anita gets ready to go to court.

18. When she arrives at court she feels a bit nervous.

19. Inside the court the police officer goes over what she said about the man.

20. Anita has to wait a long time. Her friend waits with her.

21. At last it is her turn to go in. There are lots of other people in court. The person on the highest chair is the judge. The judge and the barristers wear wigs and gowns. The jury wear ordinary clothes.

22. Anita can see the defendant. He is standing at the back of the courtroom.

23. Anita promises to tell the truth.

24. Anita's barrister stands up to ask her some questions. This barrister seems helpful and friendly. Anita feels quite calm.

25. Then the man's barrister starts asking Anita questions. The barrister's job is to make sure Anita is really telling the truth. Sometimes the barrister is not friendly.

26. Anita feels confused and upset. The questions are difficult to answer. She tells the judge she doesn't understand. She remembers what the police officer told her: "Just keep telling the truth."

27. The questions to Anita are over. She will not be asked to say anything else, even if she wants to. The judge says she can stay and listen to the other witnesses. She asks to go home. She does not want to listen to them.

28. The defendant promises to tell the truth.

29. He has to answer questions just like Anita has done.

30. Both barristers ask him questions.

31. When all the questioning is over, the judge talks to the jury. He asks if they are sure that the defendant has done something wrong. If they are sure then they must find him guilty. Then the judge will decide what will happen to the man. If the jury are not sure what happened they must say the defendant is not guilty. In this story we do not tell you what the judge decides. What do you think will happen?

32. When Anita wants to remember going to court she can read the book.

At court

Here are some of the people you might meet or hear about in court.

Victim

A victim is someone who has been hurt, or who thinks that someone has done something wrong to them. They can go to court to tell the judge what happened. The judge will see if something is wrong and try to put it right.

Witness

A witness has seen or heard something important, or they may be a victim themselves. First they must tell the police. Much later they can tell a judge and jury. This is called going to court.

Defendant

A defendant is a person who has done something wrong, or who someone else thinks has done something wrong. The defendant has to go to court to tell the judge what happened. The judge will try to sort it out.

Judge

The judge is in charge of what happens in court. His job is to try and make sure everything is fair.

Barristers

  A barrister is a lawyer who presents your case in court. The defendant and the victim will have a barrister each.

Prosecutor

This is the person who decides whether a case is going to court after the police have taken statements from the victim, witnesses and defendant. The prosecutor works for the Crown Prosecution Service.

Jury

These are 12 ordinary men and women who listen carefully to what everyone says. At the end they will have to say what they think really happened.

Usher

 The usher works in the court and knows where everyone should go.

These are some words you might hear in court

Guilty

Someone is called guilty if it is proved in court that they did something wrong.

Not guilty

Someone is called not guilty if it is proved in court that they did not do anything wrong. Sometimes they are called not guilty if the jury are not sure what really happened.

Verdict

At the end of the trial or court case, the jury give their decision about whether someone is guilty or not. This is called the verdict.

Special measures

This story can help you understand and talk about what happens when you give evidence (tell your story) in court, how it may make you feel, and some of the support that is available to make the process easier.

Since this book was first published, the law in England and Wales about how vulnerable witnesses give evidence has changed to introduce more supports, called special measures. Some special measures are included in our story *Supporting Victims*.

Special measures are:

- using an intermediary to help the witness understand questions and to help the court understand the witness's answers

- live television link between the courtroom and another room where the witness gives evidence

- people in the court taking off their wigs and gowns

- screens used around the witness box so that the witness does not see the defendant

- the video recording of the witness's statement to the police – this is shown to the court.

Aids to communication can also be used to support witnesses in police interviews and in court. Aids include pencil and paper, pictures, symbol systems and signing.

Sometimes, members of the public are asked to leave the courtroom when the witness gives evidence. This measure can only be used in cases of sexual offences or when someone has tried, or might try, to frighten the witness.

Intermediary

The intermediary helps witnesses when they speak to the police and when they answer questions in court.

If the witness does not understand a question, the intermediary can ask for the question to be made simpler. If the witness's answers are hard to understand, the intermediary tells the court what the witness said.

If the witness needs a break, the intermediary asks the court.

Intermediaries are independent and do not ask their own questions or put forward their own views in court. They are not police, lawyers, appropriate adults or supporters. Their duty is to the court.

Live television link

A live television link means the witness can give evidence from outside the courtroom. The witness can sit in a private room away from the courtroom and give their evidence and answer questions through a live television link to the courtroom. The witness will be able to see and hear the person speaking in the courtroom and those in the courtroom can see and hear the witness on a television screen.

The court usher sits with the witness in the television link room. The intermediary and/or a supporter may sit with the witness as well.

The video-recorded interview

When the witness tells the police what they know, it is recorded on a videotape. The video will be shown in the courtroom at the time of the trial.

The video can be used as the first part of the witness's evidence in court. If some things are not clear in the video, the lawyers can ask the witness questions. A television link might be used for this.

Taking wigs off

The judge and lawyers can be asked to take off their wigs and gowns. Some witnesses prefer to see these people without the wigs and gowns. Other witnesses want them to keep them on.

Screen used around the witness box

Screens can be placed around the witness box. This way the witness does not see, and cannot be seen by, the person who is accused of doing the crime.

Evidence in private

The court can be cleared of most people, but legal representatives and some other people must be allowed to stay.

Useful resources

Services in the UK

Victim Support
Victim Support is the national service for crime victims, witnesses, their families and friends. A range of services is offered by Victim Support, whether or not a crime has been reported. Victim Support provides information, practical help and emotional support to people who have experienced a crime, and to their families and friends. After a crime has been committed, a Victim Support volunteer can visit the victim at home to offer support and someone to talk to in confidence about the crime.

All criminal courts in England and Wales now have a Witness Service, managed by Victim Support. Trained personnel help victims, witnesses and their families and friends at court by showing them round the court before the hearing, supporting them on the day, giving information about court procedures, and arranging further help after court. Where an intermediary is appointed, the Witness Service can assist the intermediary by explaining court procedures. The intermediary can assist the Witness Service to communicate with the witness.

For information about how to contact your local Victim Support or Witness Service call the free national supportline.
Supportline: 08 08 16 89 111
www.victimsupport.org.uk

Respond
Respond offers assessment and treatment to people with learning disabilities who are victims and/or perpetrators of sexual abuse, and advice, training and consultancy to carers and professionals.
Helpline: 0808 808 0700
www.respond.org.uk

The **Law Society** supports and represents all solicitors practising across England and Wales with the aim of protecting everyone's right to have access to justice. They produce advice and guidance on good practice and management. Many solicitors' firms have legal advisors (legal representatives). These are non-solicitors who go to police stations to support people under arrest.
www.lawsociety.org.uk

The **Solicitor's Regulation Authority (SRA)** is an independent regulatory body created by the Law Society. They offer advice on finding and using a solicitor or what to do if you are having problems with your solicitor.
www.sra.org.uk

Independent Police Complaints Commission (IPCC)
This is an organisation that regulates the police complaints system across England and Wales. They have several easy read guides about their services, including how to make a complaint about the police and what to do if you are unhappy about the way your complaint was dealt with.
www.ipcc.gov.uk/page/alternative-formats

46

Association of Child Abuse Lawyers (ACAL)
ACAL offers practical support for lawyers and other professionals working for adults and children who have been abused.
www.childabuselawyers.com
A page on the ACAL website describes for survivors of abuse what they might expect to get from lawyers: www.childabuselawyers.com/survivors

Community Learning Disability Teams (CLDTs)
These are specialist multidisciplinary teams that support adults with learning disabilities and their families and other care-givers. They usually include nurses, clinical psychologists, and psychiatrists and others, such as speech and language therapists, occupational therapists and physiotherapists. They sometimes also have social workers and psychotherapists. You can usually find out about your local CLDT through your GP or your Council's website.

Written materials and online resources

Fair Access to Justice?: support for vulnerable defendants in the criminal courts. Produced by the **Prison Reform Trust**, this report outlines the special measures that are available to support witnesses and victims with a learning disability to understand and cope with appearing in court. This document will be particularly useful to frontline staff working in the criminal justice system and the NHS.
www.prisonreformtrust.org.uk/Publications/ItemId/156/vw/1

The **Advocates' Gateway** contains a number of toolkits providing evidence-based 'good practice' guidance when preparing for trial in cases where the defendant and/or a witness is someone with communication needs, such as a person with a learning disability or autism.
www.theadvocatesgateway.org

What's My Story? A free guide to using intermediaries to help vulnerable witnesses. Published by the **Office of Criminal Justice Reform**.
www.autism.org.uk/~/media/nas/documents/living-with-autism/whats_my_story.ashx

How to use a solicitor in England and Wales is an easy read guide produced by the **Law Society** to support solicitors' clients to understand how to access and work with them.
www.lawsociety.org.uk/for-the-public/documents/easy-read-guide-how-to-use-a-solicitor/

Abuse is Bad. By Speak Up Self-Advocacy. A DVD, produced by **Speak Up Self-Advocacy**, to give people with learning disabilities information about abuse. Copies can be ordered from the Friendly Resource catalogue.
www.friendlyresource.org.uk/

Abuse in Care? A practical guide to protecting people with learning disabilities from abuse in residential services. A guide offering information for health and social care staff.
www2.hull.ac.uk/fass/pdf/Abuse%20in%20Care%202.pdf

Social Care Institute for Excellence:
Protecting adults at risk: London multi-agency policy and procedures to safeguard adults from abuse. A guide to how organisations should work together to prevent abuse and harm.
Safeguarding adults at risk of harm: A legal guide for practitioners. An in-depth guide to the legal framework for safeguarding adults.
These guides are available from:
www.scie.org.uk/adults/safeguarding/policies

Mencap's report *Behind Closed Doors* (2001) showed that the law did not provide sufficient protection against assault for vulnerable people with severe learning disabilities. The Sexual Offences Act 2003 changed the law so that offences include sexual activity with someone who does not have the capacity to consent.
www.mencap.org.uk/sites/default/files/documents/2008-03/behind_closed_doors.pdf

Surviving Sexual Abuse – what you can do if you think you have been sexually abused. An easy read guide produced by **Enable Scotland** that explains what you can do if you have been sexually abused, and where you can get help and support. A guide for family carers and support staff, *Unlocking sexual abuse and learning disabilities*, is also available. Both guides are free to download:
www.enable.org.uk/families/Over 18/Pages/Dealing-with-abuse.aspx

Related titles in the Books Beyond Words series

Supporting Victims (2007) by Sheila Hollins, Kathryn Stone and Valerie Sinason, illustrated by Catherine Brighton. Polly is the victim of an assault. The book shows her experience as a witness at court, outlining the support and special measures that help her to give evidence.

You're under Arrest (2016, 2nd edition) by Sheila Hollins, Isabel Clare and Glynis Murphy, illustrated by Beth Webb. Dave is accused of a crime and placed under arrest. At the police station, Dave meets a custody officer and the solicitor who will help him.

You're on Trial (2016, 2nd edition) by Sheila Hollins, Glynis Murphy and Isabel Clare, illustrated by Beth Webb. Dave goes to trial at the Magistrates' Court. This book shows what a Magistrates' Court is like, and follows Dave as he works with his solicitor and answers questions in court. It can be used flexibly for different crimes and verdicts.

When Dad Hurts Mum (2014) by Sheila Hollins, Patricia Scotland and Noëlle Blackman, illustrated by Anne-Marie Perks. After her dad is violent towards her mum, Katie is sad and distracted at college. Her teacher supports the family to get the help of an Independent Domestic Violence Advocate and the police. Katie and her mum are kept safe. Katie's dad is court-ordered to join a group to stop his abusive behaviour.

Finding a Safe Place from Abuse (2015) by Sheila Hollins, Patricia Scotland and Noëlle Blackman, illustrated by Anne-Marie Perks. Katie meets David and falls in love. She moves in with him, but the relationship turns difficult and dangerous when David begins to steal her money and hurt her. Katie quickly gets help through her GP. After a stay in a refuge, Katie begins a new life with a new sense of confidence.

Mugged (2002, 2nd edition) by Sheila Hollins, Christiana Horrocks and Valerie Sinason, illustrated by Lisa Kopper. This book tells the story of Charlie who is attacked in the street. The pictures show how Charlie is helped by speedy police action, Victim Support and back-up from friends, family and supporters.

Sonia's Feeling Sad (2011) by Sheila Hollins and Roger Banks, illustrated by Lisa Kopper. Sonia is feeling so sad that she shuts herself off from her family and friends. She agrees to see a counsellor and gradually begins to feel better.

Ron's Feeling Blue (2011, 2nd edition) by Sheila Hollins, Roger Banks and Jenny Curran, illustrated by Beth Webb. Ron is depressed and has no interest in doing things. With the help of his GP and family he begins to feel better.

Jenny Speaks Out (2015, 3rd edition) by Sheila Hollins and Valerie Sinason, illustrated by Beth Webb. Jenny feels unsettled when she moves into a new home in the community. Her carer and friends sensitively help Jenny to unravel her painful past as a victim of sexual abuse, and begin a slow but positive healing process.

Bob Tells All (2015, 2nd edition) by Sheila Hollins and Valerie Sinason, illustrated by Beth Webb. Bob has moved to a group home, but his erratic behaviour and terrifying nightmares unsettle the other people living there. A social worker sensitively helps Bob unravel his painful past as a victim of sexual abuse. Bob discovers that talking with people he can trust begins a slow, but positive, healing process.

I Can Get Through It (2009, 2nd edition) by Sheila Hollins, Christiana Horrocks and Valerie Sinason, illustrated by Lisa Kopper. This book tells the story of a woman whose life is suddenly disturbed by an act of abuse. It shows how with the help of friends and counselling, the memory of the abuse slowly fades.

Books Beyond Words

A wide range of other titles is available in this series. See www.booksbeyondwords.co.uk.

Authors and artist

Sheila Hollins is Emeritus Professor of Psychiatry of Disability at St George's, University of London, and sits in the House of Lords. She has been President of the Royal College of Psychiatrists, and of the British Medical Association and the College of Occupational Therapists, and chair of the BMA's Board of Science. She is founding editor, author and Executive Chair of Books Beyond Words, and a family carer for her son who has a learning disability.

Valerie Sinason is an Adult Psychoanalyst and Child Psychotherapist, and specialises in disability, trauma and abuse. She is Director of the Clinic of Dissociative Studies and President of the Institute of Psychotherapy and Disability. She is a poet and writer, and had a grandmother with a learning disability.

Beth Webb is the artist who helped develop the very first Beyond Words books, linking emotionally-keyed colours with clear body language to enhance the simple illustrations. She is also a children's author and a professional storyteller.

Dedication

To Nicky for being so brave.

Acknowledgments

Books Beyond Words remains indebted to everyone who gave their time so generously in the preparation of the first edition of this book and thanks authors of related titles whose experience and insights have contributed to the revisions in this edition.

Our thanks are due to Kathryn Stone, Greg Barry, Sophie Bird, James Churchill, Isabel Clare, Ann Craft, Elaine Crick, Peter Dawson, Nigel Hollins, Christiana Horrocks, Joyce Plotnikoff, Nicole Roberts, Anne Stasyshyn, Lianne Webber and Chris Williams. Thanks are also due to Avon & Somerset Constabulary, Julie Boniface, Ivan Boniface, Anita Conroy, Monica Kelly, Freda Macey and the staff at Taunton Crown Court. Special mention must be made of the outstanding professional help given by Elaine Crick of the Derbyshire Constabulary. The first edition of *Going to Court* would not have been possible without generous grants from Home Office and the Department of Health.

We are grateful to the Law Society Charity for their generous funding for the second edition of this book.

Beyond Words: publications and training

Books Beyond Words are stories for anyone who finds pictures easier than words. A list of all Beyond Words publications, including print and eBook versions of Books Beyond Words titles, and where to buy them, can be found on our website:

www.booksbeyondwords.co.uk

Workshops for family carers, support workers and professionals about using Books Beyond Words are provided regularly in London, or can be arranged in other localities on request. Self-advocates are welcome. For information about forthcoming workshops see our website or contact us:

email: admin@booksbeyondwords.co.uk

Video clips showing our books being read are also on our website and YouTube channel: www.youtube.com/user/booksbeyondwords and on our DVD, *How to Use Books Beyond Words*.

How to read this book

There is no right or wrong way to read this book. Remember it is not necessary to be able to read the words.

1. Some people are not used to reading books. Start at the beginning and read the story in each picture. Encourage the reader to hold the book themselves and to turn the pages at their own pace.

2. Whether you are reading the book with one person or with a group, encourage them to tell the story in their own words. You will discover what each person thinks is happening, what they already know, and how they feel. You may think something different is happening in the pictures yourself, but that doesn't matter. Wait to see if their ideas change as the story develops. Don't challenge the reader(s) or suggest their ideas are wrong.

3. Some pictures may be more difficult to understand. It can help to prompt the people you are supporting, for example:

- Who do you think that is?
- What is happening?
- What is he or she doing now?
- How is he or she feeling?
- Do you feel like that? Has it happened to you/ your friend/ your family?

4. You don't have to read the whole book in one sitting. Allow people enough time to follow the pictures at their own pace.

5. Some people will not be able to follow the story, but they may be able to understand some of the pictures. Stay a little longer with the pictures that interest them.

56